What did I come upstairs for?

for:

May God bless your life richly!

from:

Young people take pride in their strength,
but the grey hairs of wisdom are even more beautiful.

Proverbs 20:29

(Contemporary English Version)

What did I come upstairs for?

I will remember your great deeds, LORD; I will recall the wonders you did in the past.
Psalm 77:11 (GNB)

•

I switch on the kettle to make a cup of tea and then decide to empty the tumble drier while it comes to the boil. Out come 5 shirts. If I give them a good shake and put them straight on to hangers they won't need much ironing. Hmm! No hangers to be seen. I rush upstairs to raid the wardrobes for unemployed hangers, gathering up a hairbrush to return to my daughter's bedroom, an abandoned sweatshirt for my son and half a dozen other miscellaneous items from the bottom of the stairs. I dump everything in the relevant bedrooms and notice that the laundry basket is overflowing. I grab the basket, fill it with grubby socks and whatnot and return to the kitchen.

As I'm loading the washing machine, I notice that the tumble drier is still full of shirts that are slowly getting more creased as they wait to be unloaded. Bother, I knew I'd forgotten something, time to go back upstairs!

On reaching the landing for the second time I hear the tap dripping in the bathroom and someone has left the light on too. I turn them off and return to the landing. '*Now what did I come upstairs for? To fetch the washing? No, I did that last time. To put things away? Don't think so*.' I'm going to have to retrace my steps, just to find out why I came upstairs.

Returning to the kitchen, I look around, why did I go upstairs? I spot the kettle, recently boiled and still gently steaming, maybe I'll make a cup of tea while I endeavour to remember why I went upstairs!

Does this sound familiar? Well then, perhaps you too have reached muddle-age! The stage between middle age and old age when your memory sometimes needs rebooting. Don't fret – we all do it!

Apparently scientific studies reveal that normal, healthy people can suffer up to thirty lapses of the '*What did I come upstairs for*?' type every week. It's a symptom of BLS.

Hooray! I'm perfectly normal – I'm just suffering from Busy Life Syndrome. I'm not forgetful, I just have too much to remember.

Now why did I tell you this story? I simply can't remember. However, we've filled this book with quips, quotes and anecdotes about the joys of being 'matured to perfection' and we hope that you'll enjoy them. JM

Thank you Lord that I am fearfully and wonderfully made.
In the busy-ness of life, when I'm inclined to forget other things,
help me to always remember the good things you have done for me.

These days I spend a lot of time thinking about the hereafter. I go somewhere to get something and then I wonder, 'What on earth am I here after?'

•

Arthur, aged 88, has a problem with his house. It has two stories. It has stairs. When he uses the stairs, Arthur stops midway to catch his breath. His main problem is that, when he is ready to start again, Arthur is unable to remember whether he was going upstairs or downstairs.

In the bag!

You have looked deep into my heart, LORD, and you know all about me.

Psalm 139:1 (CEV)

•

Have you tried these new super-fast, fully automatic, self-service tills at the supermarket? They really make the whole shopping experience swifter and more fun, don't they? I wish!

One day when the queues at the regular checkout were a little long, I decided that despite my muddle-aged status I would attempt to learn a new skill!

'*Touch the screen to start scanning*,' intoned the voice. '*Beep*!' I swiped the first item and dropped it into the carrier bag, then a second, so far so good. My third item was a box of eggs, so I positioned these a little more carefully in my carrier bag...

'*Unidentified object in the bagging area*!' trilled the automated voice.

'*How rude*,' I thought. '*That's no way to talk to customers*.'

'*Please wait for assistance*,' continued the disembodied voice. I waited... then I waited some more... Apparently the machine had been confused by the weight of my hands placing the eggs in the bag. Hmm!

Finally, all the shopping was packed into the bag and it was time to pay.

'*Please swipe your loyalty card*,' said the machine, so I waved my card across the scanner. No response. I waved it in the opposite direction. No response. I waved it fast, I waved it slowly, I waved it to and fro in quick succession.

'*Please swipe your loyalty card*,' demanded the machine insistently.

'*What do you think I'm doing?*' I muttered under my breath turning to shrug helplessly to the waiting queue building up behind. I wanted to make it clear that this hold-up was nothing to do with me. The machine was clearly at fault.

I took another look at my card and the colour suffused my cheeks, I'd been diligently swiping my library card! I stuffed it into my handbag before anyone noticed, slid a note into the machine, grabbed my change and scurried out of the store as fast as possible. Machines, huh! Give me a human being any day.

Isn't it a shame that these new self-service tills eliminate the need for any human interaction in shops? I'm happy to discuss the weather, the price of fish or even the state of the nation with a friendly face at the checkout. And after years of shopping in the same place I like to see familiar faces. They know me and I know them, even if only slightly. No matter how many times I use the automatic till, it's never, ever, going to recognise me, sympathise with me, talk to me or listen to me.

I'm so glad that God doesn't want to eliminate human interaction. '*Swipe your prayers across the scanner, now place your burdens in the bagging area...*' I don't think so! God knows us and loves us and he delights in interacting with us on a personal level. Hooray!

In the bag!

Lord, I'm so glad that you are a truly personal God and not a prayer-in-the-slot automatic machine. You delight in working with your children, help me to include you in every aspect of my life.

Quips and QUOTES

The three ages of man: youth, middle age and 'My word, you do look well'.

Anon

•

Age is an issue of mind over matter. If you don't mind, it doesn't matter.

Mark Twain *1835–1910, American author*

•

Everything slows down with age,
except the time it takes cake and ice cream to reach your hips.

John Wagner *1949–present day, Scottish writer of comics*

•

As a graduate of the Zsa Zsa Gabor School of Creative Mathematics,
I honestly do not know how old I am.

Erma Bombeck *1927–1996, American columnist*

•

To be seventy-years-young is sometimes far more cheerful and hopeful
than to be forty-years-old.

Oliver Wendell Holmes *1809–1894, American author*

Youth is a wonderful thing. What a crime to waste it on children.

George Bernard Shaw *1856–1950, Irish playwright*

Father and daughter: Greta Chang

To baldly go; ship-shape and bristle fashion

Indeed, the very hairs of your head are all numbered.

Luke 12:7 (NIV)

•

You never forget your first bristle.

I was rubbing my chin thoughtfully when I felt it. Something sharp and springy was pricking my fingertip. I rushed to the bathroom mirror and squinted anxiously at my chin. A solitary black whisker had sprouted overnight. Grabbing the tweezers, I seized the bristle firmly by its root and tugged. It was a stubborn beast. Finally, it was out and I gazed at the unwanted whisker in horrified fascination. So thick! So strong! I was almost proud to have produced a hair of such resilience.

God has a strange sense of humour, I've decided. While women wrestle with unwanted hair on the lower half of their face, men bemoan the loss of hair from the top half of theirs.

Mornings in the muddle-aged couple's bathroom finds the lady of the house searching for newly sprouted bristles, debating whether to just let them grow and make some money as the bearded lady in a travelling circus, while Sir pats his comb-over and assesses the distance between the first strand of hair and his eyebrows. Has it increased noticeably since last week?

Despite this joke at our expense, God tells us not to worry. He notices when a sparrow falls from the sky and he has, he assures us, numbered every hair on our head. Our future with him is secure. Of course we will age. Of course we will meet with adversity during our lifetime, but nothing can change the final outcome. Our Creator God cares deeply for us and nothing on Earth or in Heaven can separate us from his love.

There's no point splitting hairs about *that*, now, is there?

Ship-shape and bristle fashion

Why are we so vain about our looks, Father? Why do we worry unnecessarily about a few hairs lost or gained when we're assured of your watchful presence over us? Help us to relax and to accept ourselves as we are, whatever stage of life we're at.

Forty (or do I mean four hundred?) winks

Therefore keep watch because you do not know when the owner of the house will come back... If he comes suddenly, do not let him find you sleeping. ...Watch!

Mark 13:35-37 (NIV)

•

Once upon a time, I only used to sleep during the day if I was ill.

Then, one day, Middle Age came knocking at my door and not wishing to appear rude, I invited it to come in and have a cup of tea. It must have been when we were shaking hands that I caught the cat-napping bug. As a result, I started succumbing to quick

five-minute dozes. This has inexplicably increased to daily doses of shut-eye lasting anything up to an hour-and-a-half. Especially in front of the TV. Even – dare I admit it? – when it's not switched on.

My weak spot is after work when I've walked the dogs and pootled around on the computer. '*I'll just have a little rest before my husband comes home*,' I tell myself. Before I know it, the dogs are running up and down, barking with excitement as they greet the Master of the House.

"Have you been asleep?" he asks, looking around and sniffing the air in the vain hope that tea might be ready. "Urrrghhhh... just resting," I say, wiping dribble from the side of my face and wondering if it's six in the morning or the evening and will I be able to stagger to the kitchen let alone rustle up a half-decent meal?

Well, we know what Jesus had to say about being caught napping; take another look at the verse we started with. It's disturbingly easy to slip in and out of spiritual consciousness. It happens when we get swept along by all that's happening in life and forget – or decide we're too weary – to spend time with God and hear what he has to say. Before we know it, days, weeks, months have passed and God has been pushed to the very edge of the picture. If we're not careful, he can slip completely from the frame and we may find ourselves compromising our beliefs.

How do we overcome distance and weariness? It's a matter of discipline. By making a determined effort to include God in all aspects of life, we stay close to him and will be alert to even his softest whisper. AC

Father God, help us to stay spiritually awake so we may never be caught napping. When we are weary, help us rest in your love, safe from temptation and apathy. Amen.

I don't feel old. I don't feel anything till noon. That's when it's time for my nap.

Bob Hope, *1903–2003 British-American actor and comedian*

Quips and QUOTES

Age does not diminish the extreme disappointment
of having a scoop of ice cream fall from the cone.

Jim Fiebig

•

Age is something that doesn't matter,
unless you are a cheese.

Billie Burke *1884–1970, American actress*

Youth would be an ideal state if it
came a little later in life.

Herbert Asquith *1881–1947,*
English poet and lawyer

•

Children are a great comfort to us in our old age,
and they help us reach it faster too.

Anon

•

I intend to live forever, or die trying.

Groucho Marx *1890–1977,*
American comedian and film star

Rainbow road: Christine Wyl

Cherish all your happy moments;
they make a fine cushion for your old age.
Christopher Morley *1890–1957, American playwright*

Uni-versally accepted

Stand and shout praises to your LORD, the eternal God! Praise his wonderful name, though he is greater than words can express.

Nehemiah 9:5 (CEV)

•

"I'm going to Uni, next year," he said.

Uni what? I thought ungraciously. *Unicycle from John O'Groats to Lands' End? Unilaterally disarm the entire population of the Isle of Wight? Unicorn husbandry classes on Wednesday evenings?*

I cringe at the current trend for shortening perfectly good words. It offends my love of language. Well, the language that I grew up with, to be accurate. 'University' was good enough for my generation, so why isn't it now, I ponder grumpily? Can't modern students pronounce it? Do more than two syllables render them exhausted, perhaps? *"I'm going to Univer..... Zzzzz..."*

Glasgow University: Jill Bain

Such cynicism is bad for my middle-aged soul, I'm sure. I'm just as bad as those people who criticise contemporary hymns and styles of worship. *"These new 'hymns',"* they tut, *"they don't reverence God like the old ones. And all these modern translations of the Bible; they're not the same as the good old King James."*

I feel obliged to gently point out that 'old' hymns were new songs, once. I daresay the traditionalists of their day could barely disguise their disdain when John and Charles Wesley belted out their latest tunes in the 1700s. And, Jesus certainly didn't speak in the 'thees and thous' of the 16th century when he lived on Earth, hard though it is for some to believe.

All Bible translations are worthy if they connect with the people of their time and culture and make God real and accessible. And all forms of genuine worship are pleasing to God. He doesn't prefer our use of traditional versions of the Bible over contemporary ones any more than he is likely to pay more attention to someone singing a Graham Kendrick song than to someone belting out a Wesley hymn. It's the sincerity of our heart that matters, not the actual words we employ.

Have you heard the new, succinct mealtime grace that's popular amongst the youth?

'Ta Pa.'

I'm sure God laughs at that one, and is glad they remember to say thank you – in their own unique way.

Thank you or ta, thou or you, uni or university; what does it matter as long as the words are sincere and understood?

AC

Lord, I'm so glad you accept our prayers and praise in any and every language. In you there is no wrong or right way to worship. Thank you for the gift of words and the variety of ways we have of expressing our love for you. Amen.

Comfort at a s-t-r-e-t-c-h

Is not wisdom found among the aged? Does not long life bring understanding?

Job 12:12 (NIV)

●

Remember those halcyon days when the only elasticated garments we allowed past our hips were knickers and tights? Days when belts kept our trousers in situ and the tighter and more uncomfortable they were, the better we looked. Or at least we thought we did.

Ah, the folly of youth! Now we know better, of course. Those elasticated 'slacks' we once sneered at have now attained 'must-have' status. I find myself inexorably drawn to them in clothes shops.

The benefits are manifold. So comfy. So forgiving. So liberating. Did I really used to think they were for people who no longer cared about their appearance? How shallow of me! Nothing sloppy about a nice black velour two-piece, I'll have you know. Those trousers can hide a multitude of sins, from knobbly knees to heavy calves to podgy ankles (delete as applicable). As for the tops, they're usually hoodies aren't they? Very trendy. Nope, you can't beat a good leisure suit, I say.

And then there's footwear. Why teeter around in foot-cramping, toe-pinching, back-aching, neck-breaking stilettos when you can enjoy the comfort and freedom of soft, gentle loafers and moccasins? Not forgetting the blissful experience of easing into a pair of slippers. Is there anything nicer than coming home from work in the winter months and slipping straight out of work clothes into pyjamas, dressing gown and slippers, I ask myself? (Well okay, there are several things nicer, but you get my drift...)

It takes maturity to realise that comfort is more important than back-breaking, stomach-squeezing, toe-pinching fashion. Equally, being a Christian shows maturity. When we choose to follow Christ we are saying, '*I don't care what my peers think. I'm sick of struggling alone, fighting a losing battle to make sense of life, love and the universe. I'm mature enough to ask God for help when I need it. I know what matters in life!*'

God doesn't promise us an easy time when we follow him, but when life throws rotten eggs and tomatoes at us, we know who to turn to for help and reassurance.

Now, that's what I call wisdom! 

Comfort at a stretch

Lord, you are so patient with us. You let us strut around in the world, trying to be big and clever but as soon as we see the error of our ways you are there to ease our burdens and provide rest for our weary souls. Thank you, so very, very much.

Quips and QUOTES

Grow old along with me! The best is yet to be…

Robert Browning *1812–1889, English poet*

•

Anyone who stops learning is old, whether at twenty or eighty.

Henry Ford *1863–1947, American businessman*

•

We are always the same age inside.

Gertrude Stein *1874–1946, American writer*

•

Growing old is mandatory; growing up is optional.

Chili Davis *1960–present day, Jamaican former baseball player*

•

It's sad to grow old, but nice to ripen.

Brigitte Bardot *1934–present day, French actress and model*

•

There was no respect for youth when I was young, and now that I am old, there is no respect for age – I missed it coming and going.

J.B. Priestley *1894–1984, English writer*

You can't turn back the clock. But you can wind it up again.

***Bonnie Prudden** 1914–2011, American writer*

Stockbridge clock: Joseph Proctor

Memory malfunctions

Anyone who listens to the word but does not do what it says is like someone who looks at his face in a mirror and, after looking at himself, goes away and immediately forgets what he looks like.

James 1:23-24. (NIV)

•

Sometimes I scare myself.

I'll be driving along, minding my own business, when suddenly I realise that I've absolutely no idea where I'm going. Usually, it's when I've been waiting at a certain set of traffic lights where there are three options to choose from – left, right, or straight ahead. I'm so used to going straight ahead to go to work, that I find myself halfway there before realising it's Saturday and I'm supposed to be at the supermarket. Another time, I might be having a little daydream and overshoot my destination. I did this once on the motorway and it was several miles to the next exit. I arrived at my rendezvous very late and with very little fuel in the car.

There are many activities which can become so routine that we stop thinking about why or how we do them. Driving is just one of them.

It happens to me at work. I turn around and around in the centre of the kitchen, hoping I might glimpse something that will give me a clue as to what I'm supposed to be doing. My colleagues are used to my brain-dead rotations and are quick to offer suggestions, not all of them rude, I hasten to add. I'm entitled to forget. A commercial kitchen is a hectic environment and there's only so much multi-tasking a muddle-aged woman can do. At least that's what I tell myself.

There's no such excuse for memory lapses when I go to the supermarket, however. Especially when I'm there with the sole purpose of stocking up the larder. And I deserve a *double penalty* when I've got a shopping list and still get it wrong. How come I often manage to come away without milk or bread? God isn't the only one who moves in mysterious ways, let me tell you.

Far more alarming however, is the consummate ease with which we can take our eyes off God and forget to include him in our lives. It can happen without us even realising. Allowing ourselves to be side-tracked, instead of keeping our mind on Jesus, can result in us depending more and more on our own strength. It's a slippery slope. We can soon find ourselves believing we don't need God's guidance and our relationship with him breaks down as we turn away from him.

James urges us to listen to the word of God and then to act upon it. That way we are assured of his blessing upon our lives. AC

Forget-me-nots: Judith Merrell

We all forget things every day, Lord. But as long as we remember the important things – like the fact that you love us and are ready to comfort and guide us – we're not doing too badly, are we?

"Did you ever stop to think, and forget to start again?"

Winnie the Pooh *by A.A. Milne 1882–1958, English author*

Dyeing for a change

Youth may be admired for vigor,
but gray hair gives prestige to old age.
Proverbs 20:29 (*The Message*)

•

I fancied a change, something lighter and brighter for the summer, so I invested in a small bottle that would change my hair and refresh my muddle-aged image. The label on the back of the bottle said '*Use this hair dye if you have less than 10% grey hair*.' Hmmm! So they expect me to start counting them now.

Only a few days earlier, my daughter was bending over me and kindly declared that I had 'far too many grey hairs to count', so is that more or less than 10%?

Would you like a few hairy facts? Apparently blondes average about 140,000 strands of hair, brunettes average 108,000 and poor old redheads only average 90,000. (The computer didn't even mention grey-headed folk!) I have brown hair, so this little bottle would suit me fine as long as I had less than 10,800 grey hairs.

Enough with the maths, I gave up counting, took the risk, followed the instructions on the back of the bottle and came out with a shiny, glossy head of hair. I liked the effect: it was definitely harder to see the grey hairs.

I took my husband a coffee – no comment. Checked on homework progress with the grumpy teens – no comment. I'd like to say that the family were impressed by my new image, but they didn't even notice!

The Bible assures us that grey hair is a sign of wisdom, it's prestigious and should be respected. And God knows exactly how many hairs we have on our heads and he knows what colour they are, too. In fact, God knows everything about us and he notices every detail, unlike my family!

It's quite amazing when you think about it, isn't it? God, the creator of the rivers and seas, the creator of the mountains and valleys, God the creator of the stars and planets knows every little thing about us and he loves us, too, whatever colour our hair is. What an incredible thought!

JM

Father God, thank you that you know every little detail about us and you still love us completely – it's a humbling thought.

There is only one cure for grey hair. It was invented by a Frenchman.
It is called the guillotine.

P.G. Wodehouse *1881–1975, English writer*

The youth of the present-day are quite monstrous.
They have absolutely no respect for dyed hair.

Oscar Wilde *1854–1900, Irish playwright and poet, taken from* Lady Windermere's Fan.

White as snow: Angie Sanders

Quips and QUOTES

Sport

When I was 40, my doctor advised me that a man in his 40s shouldn't play tennis.
I heeded his advice carefully and could hardly wait until I reached 50 to start again.

Hugo L. Black *1886–1971, American lawyer*

•

The only sport left to me now is hunting for my glasses.

Anon

•

Like a lot of fellows around here, I have a furniture problem.
My chest has fallen into my drawers.

Billy Casper *1931–present day, American golfer writing about golf's Senior Tour*

•

Years ago we discovered the exact point, the dead centre of middle age.
It occurs when you are too young to take up golf and too old to rush to the net.

Franklin Adams *1851–1960, American columnist*

•

Men do not quit playing because they grow old;
they grow old because they quit playing.

Oliver Wendell Holmes *1809–1894, American author*

No problem!

Whatever you do, work at it with all your heart, as working for the Lord, not for human masters... It is the Lord Christ you are serving.

Colossians 3:23-24 (NIV)

•

It's ironic, but another current trend I have a problem with is the expression, '*No problem*!' Or even worse, '*No probs*!'

"Do you want salt and vinegar?" I was asked at the fish-and-chip shop.

"Yes please," I replied.

"No problem!" was the cheerful response.

Good, I'm glad my acceptance of the service offered didn't bring the world to a grinding halt. I wasn't expecting it to be a problem. Should it be?

I work as a chef, and the supplier of our vegetable oil rings up once a fortnight to see if our stocks need replenishing.

"I'll have one drum this week please," I said recently.

"No problem!" was the happy reply.

'*I'm not surprised*,' I thought sarcastically. '*That's how it works. You run a business whereby you offer me a product in return for money. Of course it's not a problem. I'm helping you by contributing to the profitability of your business*!'

Perhaps the next time they ring I'll ask for 901 drums of oil and see what their response is. I suspect it may be along the lines of, "Um, we might have slight problem with that."

I know, I'm just a grumpy old woman. I should be delighted when people are happy in their work and have a 'can do' attitude, especially as I'm even more irritated by sullen, disinterested staff. It's horrible when you're made to feel like an unwelcome gate-crasher at a private party when you enter a shop. No one likes to be treated as if their very existence is an inconvenience, particularly when the staff are being paid to attend to the customers' needs.

Being happy in our work and in the daily tasks we undertake is a gift. Paul tells us to be willing, enthusiastic workers. Do everything as though you are working for Christ, he advises. It certainly helps. However repetitive or unglamorous the task or job might be, it can be made all the more rewarding by dealing with each task as though Jesus himself has set it for us. And in a way he has. We are all made in the image of God and whenever we serve one another, we are serving God.

AC

No problem! Aagghh!

Thank you for the opportunity to serve you through the people we meet. Let us be willing, cheerful workers for whom no act of service is a problem; after all, ultimately it's you Lord, that we seek to serve.

...whatever you did for one of the least of these brothers of mine, you did for me.
Matthew 25:40 (NIV)

A new beginning

'...For I know the plans I have for you,' declares the LORD, 'plans to prosper you and not to harm you, plans to give you hope and a future.'

Jeremiah 29:11 (NIV)

I've just been reading an article that really made me smile. It was all about a resourceful chap called Brian who used his carpentry skills to convert his mobility scooter into a Batmobile to raise money for charity. He found that he liked it so much that he kept it that way and now he always makes people smile when he heads out to the local shops. Apparently his next project is to turn a mobility scooter into a *Thunderbirds* rocket! I'd love to see it!

It's easy to approach getting older somewhat half-heartedly, but Brian reminds me that you can also approach it creatively, joyously and whole-heartedly. Retirement offers a new beginning, the chance to tackle new projects, the extra time needed to learn new skills. I still have a while to wait but I'm looking forward to it already!

Henry Ford, the founder of the motor company, said, "Anyone who stops learning is old, whether at twenty or eighty." So, when I retire, I plan to learn Italian, visit Rome and discover how to make home-made pasta. There's a whole world of mouth-watering pasta recipes out there just waiting to be sampled! *Magnifico!*

So, how about you? What are your plans and dreams?

In his senior years, Noah listened to God and built a truly magnificent ark. He was an awesome 600 years old on the day his vast boat started to float. Abraham set out with Sarah for The Promised Land when he was 75 and he was an incredible 100 years old when his son Isaac was born. Hmmm... perhaps I should go beyond learning to make pasta?

One or two of my friends have used their retirement to tackle a special God-given project. One leads an annual children's holiday club in his local church. Another friend, Jan, visits Southern Sudan for 12 weeks each year to teach English and literacy skills in a Bible school. There's no such thing as 'too old', God still has plenty of exciting projects lined up for his children, both at home and abroad.

Now there's an exciting prospect!

Lord you created me and gave me all my skills and interests. Please use the things I'm good at to do something special for you. And maybe help me to work on the things I'm not so good at, too!

There is a fountain of youth: it is your mind, your talents, the creativity you bring to your life and the lives of the people you love. When you learn to tap this source, you will have truly defeated age.

Sophia Loren *1934–present day, Italian actress*

Grow old along with me! The best is yet to be...

Robert Browning *1812–1889, English poet*

Quips and QUOTES

Everyone is the age of their heart.

Guatemalan proverb

•

There is still no cure for the common birthday.

John Glenn *1921–present day, American astronaut*

•

There is always a lot to be thankful for, if you take the time to look.
For example, I'm sitting here thinking how nice it is that wrinkles don't hurt.

Anon

•

Setting a good example for your children takes all the fun out of middle age.

William Feather *1889–1981, American Publisher*

•

Wisdom doesn't necessarily come with age.
Sometimes age just shows up all by itself.

Tom Wilson *1880–1965, American film actor*

Wise old owl: James Norton

More haste, less speed

When he knocked on the door to the courtyard, a young woman named Rhoda came to see who it was. But when she recognised his voice – Peter's voice! – she was so excited and eager to tell everyone Peter was there that she forgot to open the door and left him standing in the street.

Acts 12:12-14 (The Message)

•

One of my colleagues went out for a family meal in a posh restaurant. Grandma was with them and she really liked the restaurant and its cheerful reception area. As they waited to be seated, Gran reached out to sample the bowl of snacks on the table. "Eughh!" she choked. "These crisps are disgusting!"

"That's not surprising," said her grandson, "you're eating the pot pourri."

My mother was staying at an old friend's house and she was brushing her hair in front of the mirror when she spotted a can of hairspray. '*Just what I need*,' she thought, and quickly sprayed her fly-away hair. The disgusting smell gave away the fact that she'd liberally lacquered her hair with fly spray – the result was fly-away hair that kept flies away.

And then there's my friend, Beth, who went to the swimming pool recently and when she unrolled her towel in the changing room, she found her pyjamas inside!

Oh dear, we could blame these actions on ageing eyesight, or on a senior moment, but sometimes we simply act first and think afterwards. Only this morning I was rushing to load the dishwasher when I realised that I'd added three dirty coffee mugs to an otherwise clean dishwasher. And these mugs had dripped coffee dregs all over the bottom rack. Don't you just hate it when you do that?

I'm sure that many so-called senior moments are probably the result of trying to do things too quickly. There's a wonderful phrase in Latin which seems to fit the bill… *festina lente* or 'hurry slowly'. I like it, proceed quickly, but with caution. More haste less speed, if you like. Sometimes we're in such a hurry that we make stupid mistakes.

Tranquillity: Angie Sanders

There's a lovely Bible story in which Peter is set free from prison by an angel. Despite being shackled between two soldiers, his chains just fall off and he is able to walk right out of the prison to the house where his friends are praying that he will not receive the death sentence. Rhoda, a servant girl, goes to the door and she is so excited and amazed to hear Peter's voice that she runs back to the group to tell them the good news without actually opening the door! The trouble is, they refuse to believe her and Peter is left outside, knocking on the door for quite some time.

Sometimes the angels in heaven must fall over laughing at the crazy things we human beings do. JM

Lord, help me to slow down a little and think before I act. Sometimes I'm in such a hurry that I do the stupidest things.

Antiques in Lycra

And you yourself must be an example to them by doing good works of every kind.

Titus 2:7 (*NLT*)

•

A lunchtime Pilates group has just started in the office block behind mine. Every Wednesday lunchtime, we don T-shirts and leggings and pop to the neighbouring office for an hour of stretching and bending. Pilates is a very slow form of exercise that particularly suits my muddle-aged status. All the movements are slow and careful and aimed at improving muscle tone and flexibility.

When one of my colleagues dubbed the session *Antics in Lycra*, another misheard and assumed he said *Antiques in Lycra*. As I'm the oldest member of the group, the name seems to be appropriate. It's a case of lunchtime Pilates for seniors, where actions creak louder than words.

One lunch hour, we were all stretching our arms high in the air, first the left and then the right, stretching our biceps and triceps. I looked up to see someone watching us from the first-floor window of the office directly opposite. When I looked again, she had left her computer and was copying us, arms in the air, stretching high, a few seconds later she had two more colleagues with her, a row of three, mirroring everything we were doing! We were laughing so hard at their mimicry that it was difficult to keep going. Later, our Pilates instructor went over to invite the girls to join our group. I hope that they do, we could do with some youngsters.

Paul wrote to Titus that older believers should model good behaviour for the younger folk to copy and that he, Titus, should be a man of complete integrity, sincere in all his teaching. These verses really made me stop and think. If other people, younger believers, are watching the way I behave, I can't help wondering what kind of lessons they are learning about Christianity from me. Oh dear, all those times when I've been grumpy, critical, short tempered or impatient, I certainly hope that no one was watching and then maybe copying my example later.

JM

Lord, with age comes responsibility and that's quite a burden. When I'm about to behave in a way that lets you down, to fly off the handle or over-react, help me to stop and count to ten before I say or do anything.

Antiques in Lycra

To get back my youth I would do anything in the world, except take exercise, get up early, or be respectable.

Oscar Wilde *1854–1900, Irish playwright and poet*

The first sign of maturity is the discovery that the volume knob also turns to the left.

Jerry M. Wright

•

Age is a high price to pay for maturity.

Tom Stoppard *1937–present day, British playwright*

•

At sixteen I was stupid, confused and indecisive.
At twenty-five I was wise, self-confident, prepossessing and assertive.
At forty-five I am stupid, confused, insecure and indecisive.
Who would have supposed that maturity is only a short break in adolescence?

Jules Feiffer *1929–present day, American cartoonist*

•

You are only young once, but you can stay immature indefinitely.

Ogden Nash *1902–1971, American poet*

A restful place: Liz Edwards

Lost and found

When they did not find him, they went back to Jerusalem to look for him. After three days they found him in the temple courts, sitting among the teachers, listening to them and asking them questions. Everyone who heard him was amazed at his understanding and his answers.

Luke 2:45-47 (NIV)

•

I was delighted to sail straight into a parking space outside our local superstore the other day. It's a vast place and I frequently have to drive up and down the rows several times before I can find a space. At 8.30 a.m. on Tuesday morning though, there were plenty of spaces. This is the best time to shop, I thought smugly, as I strolled up and down the aisles.

An hour later, I emerged with my laden trolley to find a rather different scenario. The car park was now overflowing, with scarcely a space to be seen. When I parked the car it had been surrounded by empty spaces and easy to spot. Now it was a whole different picture. I pushed my trolley up one row and down another. Where had I parked the car? I took another look. It must be here somewhere. I had an appointment to go to, I really needed my trusty black Ford. Had someone stolen it? And how would I know if they had, since I couldn't remember where I'd left it?

I took a deep breath and went back to the beginning of the rows of cars to start again, walking slowly and looking carefully. I couldn't help feeling muddle-aged and stupid, and I was getting very hot under the collar. Eventually, after a good deal of stress, I found my car, quietly sitting there, minding its own business, just waiting to be found. Phew! Panic over!

This weekend, I'm off to buy a bright pink ball with dangling ribbons to attach to my aerial, then I'll be able to spot my car from a distance. No more manic car-park-searching for me!

The whole incident reminded me of the Bible story about Mary and Joseph losing Jesus. After three days of increasingly frantic searching, they returned to the Temple and found him quietly sitting there, talking to the teachers, waiting to be found, though he would not have considered himself lost.

Today, it's even easier, and completely stress-free – whenever we need Jesus he is there, he wants us to find him and he's quietly waiting for us to turn to him. So, next time you're having a stressful moment, talk to Jesus about it – he's always ready to listen. JM

Lost and found

Lord, help me to remember that you are only a prayer away,
I just need to open my mouth and you are already listening.
Help me to feel your presence in my life.

Quick question: If all is not lost, where is it?

●

Before beginning a Hunt, it is wise to ask someone what you are looking for before you begin looking for it.

Winnie the Pooh *from* Pooh's Little Instruction Book *by A.A. Milne 1882–1958*

Rendered genderless!

So there is no difference between Jews and Gentiles, between slaves and free people, between men and women; you are all one in union with Christ Jesus.

Galatians 3:28 (GNB)

A country walk: Liz Edwards

It was all straightforward when the apostle Paul wrote the verse on the left, but if he were around today he might feel as niggled as I do when it comes to being rendered genderless in worldly terms.

It was bad enough being classed as 'guys and gals' but now it seems that people can't be bothered to differentiate between male and female. Or have we become so androgynous that it's impossible to tell the genders apart?

Perhaps you've been in a restaurant enjoying a meal when the waiter comes over and enquires, "Everything all right with you guys?" *Well, no. Not really. Am I so hideously unfeminine that I'm readily mistaken for a member of the opposite sex? What happened to* 'Is everything all right Sir? Madam?' *Or even*, 'Is everything all right with your meal?'

And it's not just young people who've adopted the term, either, as I've discovered to my horror. My cringe-ometer nearly shot off the scale when someone in their late eighties smiled and asked, "Would one of you guys..." What is the world coming to?

Oh, I'm being an unreasonable grumpy old woman, I know. Nobody else seems bothered. In fact, everyone else is adjusting to new terminology happily enough, but I just can't bring myself to force out the word. Unless I'm speaking to someone called Guy or talking about Guy Fawkes, that is.

Not that God is bothered, according to Paul. Quite the opposite, in fact. In Heaven we will all be equal and there will be no need to differentiate between gender, race, status or any of the other categories that segregate and divide mankind.

Oh well, in that case, I suppose I'd better get used to it. If you can't beat 'em, join 'em, as they say.

See you, g... See you *g...uys.* AC

How wonderful it will be, Father, when all the worldly distinctions that separate us are gone and we can worship you as one, unfettered by terms and categories.

Act your shoe size not your age!

middle age is...

Middle age is when you choose your cereal for the fibre, not the toy.

Anon

•

Middle age is when we can do just as much as ever – but would rather not.

Anon

•

Middle age is when a narrow waist and a broad mind begin to change places.

Anon

•

Middle age is when your age starts to show around your middle.

Bob Hope *1903–2003, British-American actor and comedian*

•

Middle age is when your classmates are so grey and wrinkled and bald they don't recognise you.

Bennett Cerf *1898–1971, American publisher*

•

Middle age is when you're sitting at home on a Saturday night and the telephone rings and you hope it isn't for you.

Ogden Nash *1902–1971, American poet*

•

Middle age is when you've met so many people that every new person you meet reminds you of someone else.

Ogden Nash

•

Middle Age is that perplexing time of life when we hear two voices calling us, one saying, "Why not?" and the other, "Why bother?"

Sydney J. Harris *1917–1986, American writer*

What's in a name?

To everyone who is victorious I will give some of the manna that has been hidden away in heaven. And I will give to each one a white stone, and on the stone will be engraved a new name that no one understands except the one who receives it.

Revelation 2:17 (NLT)

•

Picture the scene. I'm in a queue at the dentist's/doctor's/library/wherever and it's my turn to be served.

"And what was your name?" the receptionist asks.

Time stands still and you hear my heart beating in slow motion as I contemplate telling her my maiden name. Dare I risk the anger of the restless queue behind me as I wait for her to search through the records in a vain attempt to locate my details? Will I be brave enough, when she returns empty-handed and apologetic, to suggest she might have more success if she'd asked me what my name *is* as opposed to what it was? No, I'm not that daring. I merely sigh to myself and tell her my married name. You can no longer hear my heartbeat, and time returns to normal speed.

Honestly, the older I get, the worse I become. There are far more important things to worry about than what tense someone uses when they ask me my name, but then names are so personal, aren't they? Our name gives us our sense of identity. We may lose our teeth, and our sight and hearing may deteriorate with age, but our name remains intact. No wonder it's so important.

The Bible has much to say about names. God calls us individually by name. Our names are engraved on the palm of his hand. He changed Abram's name to Abraham as a sign of covenant in the book of Genesis, and Saul became Paul upon his conversion in the book of Acts. We too, will be given a new name when we reach heaven, says John in Revelation.

Just think; when our life on Earth is over and we stand victorious before God, he will give us our own special name and we will find our ultimate identity as his son or daughter. I won't mind being asked what my name was, or is, anymore.

And my address will be 'Heaven'. Not like standing in the queue in that scene from my everyday life. Because you know what comes after asking your name, don't you? "And what was your address?"

Well, I've moved house five times in my life. Where should I start; alphabetically or chronologically? AC

Why do I get so uptight about my name, Lord? You don't want me to be so pedantic, do you? Help me to focus on the things that really matter in this life so that one day I can stand before you and receive my new name and true identity in your kingdom.

Stay in touch!

Never give up praying. And when you pray, keep alert and be thankful.
Colossians 4:2 (CEV)

•

I send emails and texts regularly, but I've never sent a Tweet. I've only Skyped a couple of times but I visit Facebook once in a while and I Google every day!

My poor grandmother would have thought I was speaking a foreign language if I had told her all this, sometimes I even confuse myself. We have so many new verbs in our language like Googling, Tweeting and Skyping that if you don't stay up to date you are very soon out of date.

Stay in touch!

When I was growing up, my sister and I would hog the phone every night talking to the school friends that we'd seen all day. Today, youngsters start texting their friends while they are still on the bus going home. My daughter once texted her friend 'Goodbye' while we were reversing off their driveway! What has become of simply talking? It's good to talk!

I have just bought a new mobile phone – it's very clever and has a voice-recognition package. Hooray, I can speak my texts, what could be easier? My first attempts at spoken texts worked really well. I said *Thank you!* or *I'll be five minutes late* and the phone reproduced my words as a text. So-o-o very clever! But then I thought I'd send my friend Di a message.

"Hi Di," I said slowly and clearly to my phone. "Does an early evening meal suit you?"

Hello Dolly! Dance an early evening mail cid stew? typed my phone. Hmmm, not quite so clever then!

I don't know, we have all these new-fangled devices that help us to stay in touch, but they all need learning, understanding and an A-level in electronic gadgetry before we can get them right. And then, if there's no signal, or we've run out of credit, or forgotten to charge the battery, they are totally useless at the very moment we need them most.

I'm so glad that God doesn't need texts, e-mails or tweets before I can talk to him. Facebook is fantastic, mobile phones are marvellous but prayer is plain perfect. All I have to do is think what I want to say and God hears, what could be simpler than that? So, I can't help wondering why I don't pray more often? JM

Lord, you've made it so easy for us to talk to you and yet I'm still hopeless at staying in touch. I'm sorry, thank you for your patience with me.

Quips and QUOTES

An archaeologist is the best husband any
woman can have: the older she gets,
the more interested he is in her.

***Agatha Christie** 1890–1976, English author*

•

Age is not a particularly interesting subject.
Anyone can get old.
All you have to do is live long enough.

***Groucho Marx** 1890–1977, American comedian*

•

You know you've reached middle age when a
doctor, not a policeman, tells you to slow down,
all you exercise are your prerogatives and it
takes you longer to rest than to get tired.

Anon

•

Don't let ageing get you down.
It's too hard to get back up.

***John Wagner** 1949–present day, Scottish comic book writer*

•

Age appears best in four things: old wood to
burn, old wine to drink, old friends to trust,
and old authors to read.

***Francis Bacon** 1909–1992, Irish artist*

Polar bear family: Charles Kinsey

When I was a boy of 14, my father was so ignorant
I could hardly stand to have the old man around.
But when I got to be 21, I was astonished at how
much the old man had learned in seven years.

Mark Twain *1835–1910, American author*

A good yarn

Finally, all of you should agree and have concern and love for each other.
You should also be kind and humble.
1 Peter 3:8 (CEV)

•

Many, many years ago my grandmother taught me to knit, but as she lived a long way away, our lessons were few and far between, so I didn't really progress further than knitting scarves for all my teddy bears. Grandma, though, was a talented knitter and she made bed socks and bed jackets, hot-water-bottle covers and cardigans for all the people she cared about. She hated the very thought of someone feeling cold and showed her concern for people by knitting for them. Very few people can knit these days and I really wish I'd paid more attention to her lessons.

Now, I've just read a story about a group of ladies knitting sweaters for penguins! You can just picture it, can't you? These penguins were caught up in an oil spillage off New Zealand and their feathers were covered in thick, black, toxic oil. The poor little chaps wanted to preen and clean their feathers, but the oil was poisonous to their systems so a group of knitting nannies from round the world made and posted tiny sweaters to keep them warm and stop them ingesting the oil while they were recovering their strength. Had she been alive today, my grandmother would have been clicking her needles fast and furiously in this good cause.

For some obscure reason the article reminded me of Tabitha in the Bible – she was always doing good things for people and looking after the poor folk in her town. She made coats and clothes and used her skill with a needle to help others. When she died, Peter visited her house and her friends, many of whom were poor widows, showed him all the clothes that she had made for them. Then Peter prayed and, by an amazing miracle, she came back to life. It's a lovely story: you'll find it in Acts, chapter 9.

Isn't it great when people use their skills and hobbies to help others? Everyone appreciates the personal touch. Now, I'm hopeless at sewing and knitting, but I've been known to arrange a few flowers to cheer a friend and I can make a passable lasagne to welcome folk round for a meal. I'm also fairly OK with a paintbrush and a roll of wallpaper, so maybe I can help people in other ways. God gave us a rich variety of skills and when we combine our efforts and add a little TLC, we can make the world a better place to be in. JM

A good yarn

Lord, help us to show your love to other people in lots of little ways. And help us to add a personal touch to show just how much we care.

Designed to help

"Do not think that I have come to abolish the Law or the Prophets; I have not come to abolish them but to fulfil them."

Matthew 5:17 (NIV)

Designed to help

No way was a computer ever going to cross our threshold, thank you very much. Not if I had anything to do with it.

"But the girls will need one once they are in secondary school," argued my technology-embracing husband.

"Humph!" was my response.

"We've managed well enough without up until now. Nothing wrong with pen and paper. They cost less, don't go wrong and are power-cut proof."

Well, that was 14 years ago, and since then more than one computer has not only been accepted by me, but actively welcomed into the house.

Where would I be without my PC? Word-processing is a doddle now. Gone is the carbon paper and corrective fluid. There's fewer screwed-up sheets of paper hitting the wastepaper basket, and less frustration and naughty words. (Unless we're talking about the printer of course, but that's another matter.)

And then there's the Internet, with a wealth of knowledge just a mouse click away. Instant access to facts and figures means that questions can be answered and queries satisfied within minutes. It's marvellous! That's not to say pen and paper and reference books are redundant. There's still something special about a handwritten letter or the smell and feel of a book.

The Jews found it hard to accept Jesus when he came to Earth. They had their rituals and long-established forms of worship and they were none-too-happy when Jesus came along and told them there was a better way. Through him, and the work of the Holy Spirit, each believer could have instant access to the heart of God. There was no longer a need to place sacrifices on altars; Jesus was the way of forgiveness, the open door between Heaven and Earth. What a massive concept for the Jews to accept! A whole new way of thinking and doing and being. They found it hard, but for those who embraced Jesus and his teaching, what a wonderful liberating gift they received!

As with everything in life, the old ways aren't necessarily the best ways. God doesn't change but neither does he stand still. AC

Lord, sometimes I'm a real dinosaur and a bit scared of new technology; help me to be open to the new ideas which enable us to learn more about the world and more about you.

Before the age of the computer a website was a spider's home,
memory was something that faded with age and a mouse
was a small furry creature with whiskers and a long tail.
Funny how things change!

Anon

Old age is...

Old age is fifteen years older than I am.

***Oliver Wendell Holmes** 1809–1894, American author*

•

Old age ain't no place for sissies.

***Bette Davis** 1908–1989, American actress*

•

Old age isn't so bad when you consider the alternative.

***Maurice Chevalier** 1888–1972, French actor*

•

Old age is like everything else.
To make a success of it, you've got to start young.

***Theodore Roosevelt** 1858–1919, 26th President of the USA*

•

Old age is an excellent time for outrage.
My goal is to say or do at least one outrageous thing every week.

***Louis Kronenberger** 1904–1980, American writer*

A balancing act

You crease me up!

Our mouths were filled with laughter, our tongues with songs of joy.

Psalm 126:2 (NIV)

•

Well, it's true Lord, you do!

I think you want us to have that many wrinkles that you won't need to open the gates of Heaven for us; St Peter will be able to fold us up and slide us in under the door.

'*Actually*,' she said, vainly patting her cheeks, '*my wrinkles aren't too bad*.' Yet. It's the one and only advantage of being well-padded – or hanging on to my puppy fat, as I prefer to call it – my skin is being pushed outwards so keeping the ravages of time at bay. I'll probably wake up tomorrow morning with a face like the Grand Canyon as a result of my vanity.

I've got some, of course. I'm not sure when the crow landed on my face (I certainly didn't feel it) but it left some nifty footprints around my eyes.

Why are we so obsessed with ageing? Or not ageing, to be more precise. Women, in particular, are at pains to retain the soft skin of youth. Magazines are peppered with adverts for lotions and creams while companies spend millions on TV advertising, attempting to convince us that their products will combat the effects of nature's clock. Why?

Ageing shows character. It shows that we have lived. We have experienced joys and sorrows, tears and love and laughter. Look at the smooth skin of a baby and you look at a blank canvas. Life has not yet drawn experience on the fresh, clean surface. But look at someone in later life and you will see a wealth of texture and experience painted in the contours of his or her face. You can almost trace the laughter lines. It's a work of art. We are all the unique product of the experiences we have been through. Why crave a face as bland and uniform as a white wall when we can smile through cheeks as beautiful and detailed as the Sistine Chapel?

Let's wear our wrinkles with pride. Especially the laughter lines.

You, Lord, are not only the Author of Life, but the Artist of Experience. What must you think of our vanity? Forgive us our foolish pride and help us to see the beauty that age, wisdom and experience reveal upon our face. Each face a work of art, designed and nurtured by you, and backlit with a smile.

Young and wrinkly

Wrinkles should merely indicate where smiles have been.

Mark Twain *1835–1910, American author*

When grace is joined with wrinkles, it is adorable.
There is an unspeakable dawn in happy old age.

Victor Hugo *1802–1885, French author*

Head in the clouds: Glynis Forbes

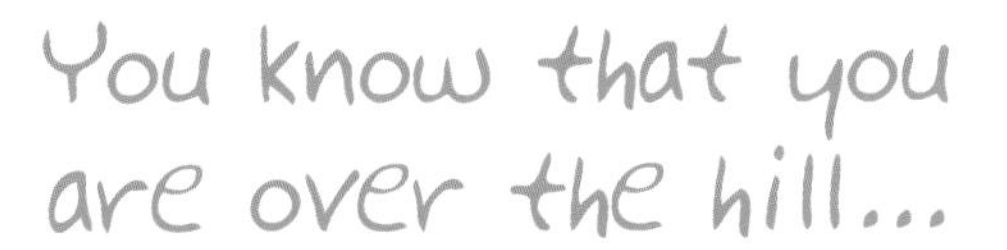

when you've seen it, done it and can't remember most of it.

●

when you'd feel nostalgic, if only you could remember what for.

●

when you keep repeating yourself.

●

when happy means an after-lunch nap…

●

when your reclining chair has more options than your car.

●

when you do the 'Hokey Cokey' you put your left hip out... and it stays out.

●

when you keep repeating yourself.

●

when the waiter asks how you'd like your steak...and you say, "Puréed".

●

when you realise that a stamp today costs more than a cinema ticket when you were young.

●

when you choose your church based on the comfort of the pews.

●

when you keep repeating yourself.